CALMING WINGS

BONNIE WILCZYNSKI, LCAT

CALMING WINGS

A Butterfly Coloring Book for Relaxation and Mindfulness

A Stress Relieving Companion for:

Seeing Creatively: How to Unlock Your Imagination
Amazon: https://a.co/d/7XkMBln

Awaken Your Inner Warrior: A Guide to Mindfulness through Meditative Neurographical Art
Amazon: https://a.co/d/6Bk0fPB

BONNIE WILCZYNSKI, LCAT

Copyright © 2025 by Bonnie Wilczynski

All rights reserved. This book or any part of it may not be reproduced or used in any way without the publisher's explicit written permission, except for brief quotations used in a book review.

Published by: Creative Visionology, 2024
Printed in the United States of America
ISBN (paperback): 979-8-9912620-4-0
Library of Congress Control Number: 2025919704

To my loving Family. I am beyond blessed to have you all.

To my Readers and Butterfly Enthusiasts, and lovers of nature, who desire transformation and mindful ways to relieve stress through the simple freedom of coloring.

CONTENTS

Introduction

Inspirational Wisdom – Ideas to Try

Like a butterfly, allow yourself to unfold in your own time.

Every wingbeat is a reminder of your freedom.

Transformation begins with a single gentle step.

Butterflies do not ask permission to evolve, and neither should your art.

Let your colors shine from within.

Trust the process of becoming.

Every moment is a chance to bloom anew.

Lightness is found when you release what weighs you down.

You are a masterpiece in progress.

Breathe deeply and let your spirit take flight.

Embrace change; it carries you to brighter skies.

Beauty is revealed in patience and time.

Your journey is as unique as your wings.

Healing happens quietly, like a cocoon transforming to fly.

Rest, restore, and rise again.

Grace flows through you when you let go.

Every shade you choose reflects your soul.

The universe whispers through your stillness.

Transformation is the art of courage.

Color your world with kindness.

Breathe in peace, breathe out love.

Spread your wings; your time has come.

Be gentle with yourself, for growth takes time.

Transformation is proof of your strength.

Let your imagination take flight.

Stillness allows beauty to emerge.

Every color holds the power to soothe your soul.

Trust the rhythm of your journey.

Within you lies infinite possibility.

Remember: you, too, are meant to fly.

Your Creativity brings beauty to the world.

Each breath is a chance to begin again.

The smallest steps lead to the greatest transformations.

Creativity is the language of the heart.

Like Butterflies, joy comes when you least expect it.

Creativity opens the door to peace.

Acknowledgements

About the Author

Inspirational Wisdom

Try these and creative Ideas, and remember to have FUN!

- Pastel Colors
- Shades of the Season
- Using Only Markers
- Use Shades of Blue
- Shades of Purple
- Use Shades of Orange
- Using Only Watercolors
- Use Warm Colors
- Using Colored Pencils
- Create a Stained-Glass Effect
- Use Primary Colors
- Use Shapes and Lines in Each Area

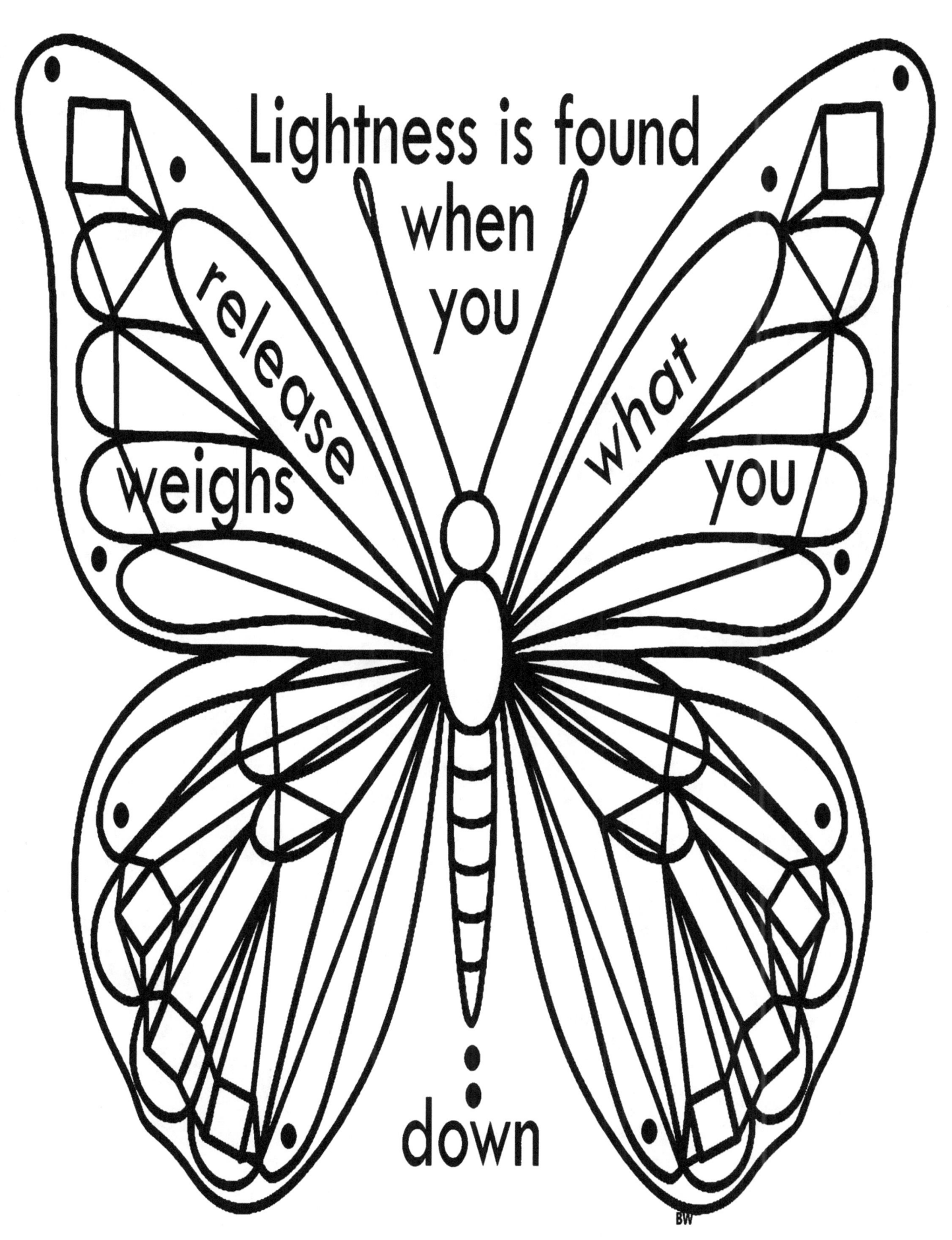

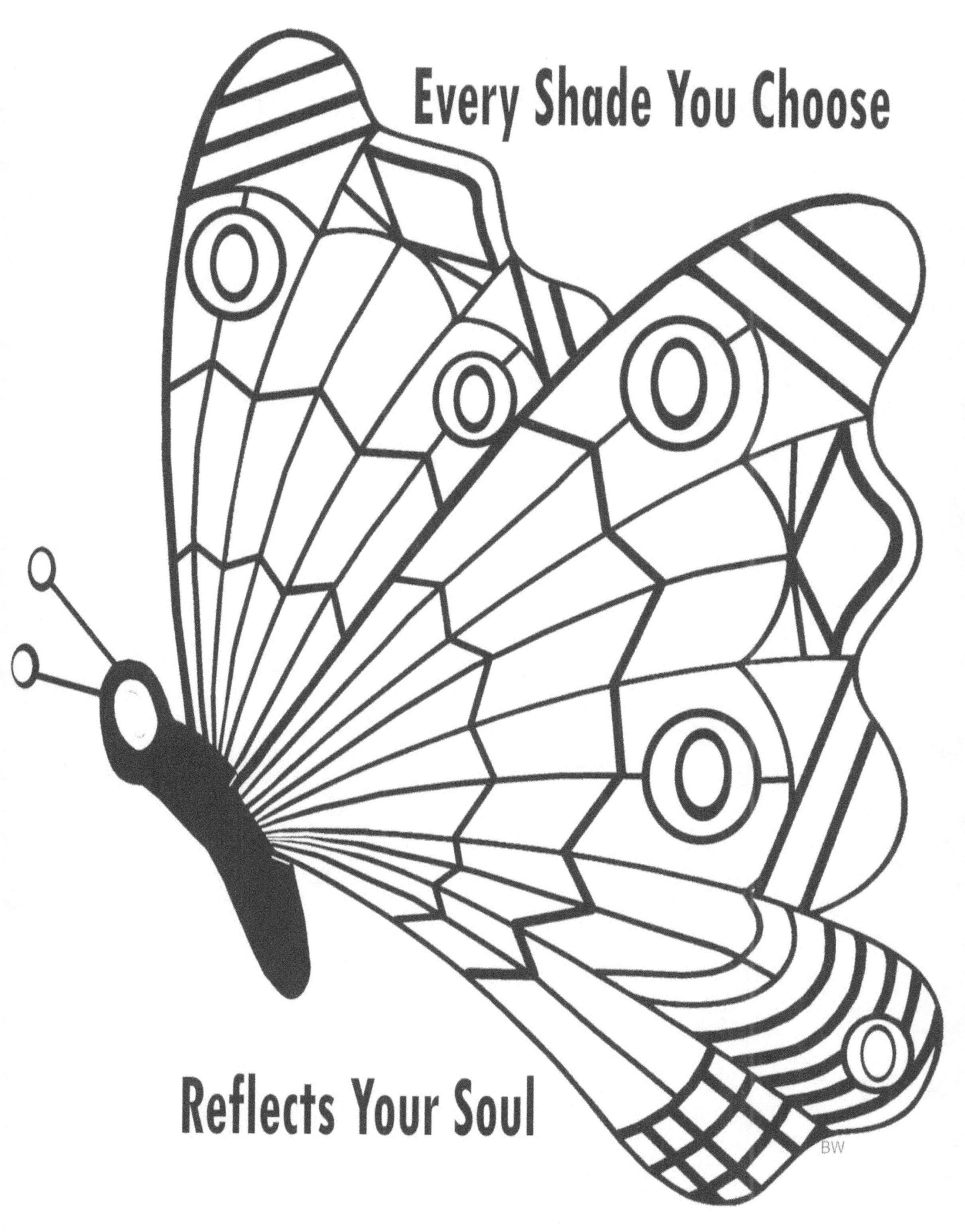

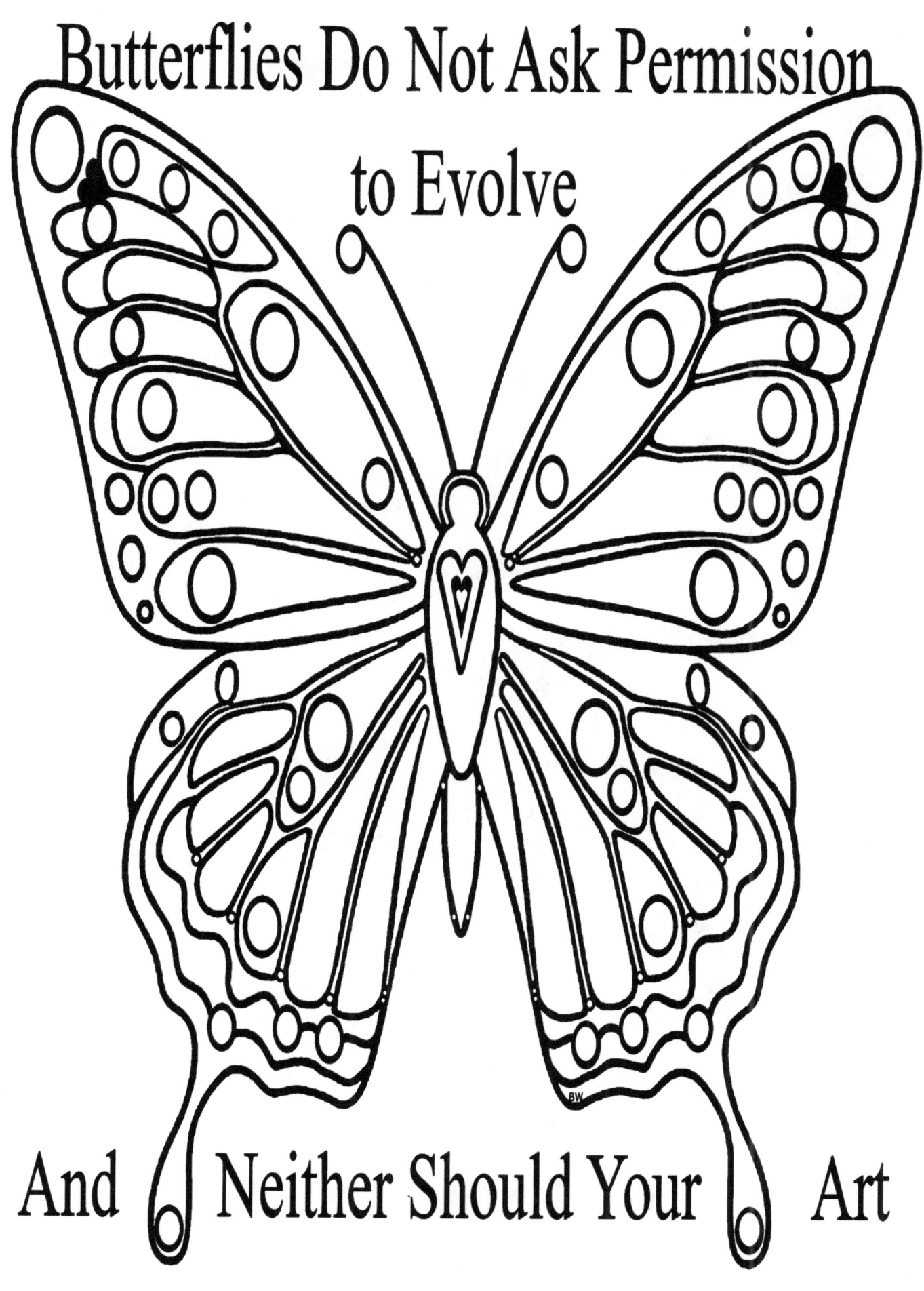

ABOUT THE AUTHOR
BONNIE WILCZYNSKI, LCAT

Bonnie Wilczynski is the Author of her successful, visionary book, Seeing Creatively: How to Unlock Your Imagination, released earlier in 2024. She also wrote and illustrated her follow-up successful mindful book, Awaken Your Inner Warrior: A Guide to Mindfulness through Meditative Neurographic Art, which was released in 2025. She has been in the "creativity business" for five decades. She is an entrepreneur, educator, artist, speaker, and Licensed Creative Arts Therapist.

Bonnie graduated with a Bachelor of Science degree in Communicative Education from California State University, Northridge. She received Early Childhood Education (ECE) certification, an art teaching certification for K-8, and a Licensed Creative Arts Therapist (LCAT) certification.

She has been an insurance underwriter, entrepreneur, small business connector, collaborator, and synergist. She is an artist, art teacher, private coach, and adult educator. Bonnie has articles published in The Beverly Hills Courier and The New Canaan Advertiser, and her artwork is on display at Central Park Fine Arts on W 57th Street in New York.

Originally from Northridge, California, Bonnie now lives with her wonderful husband in Texas. They have two happily married children and four grandchildren who are great sources of love and support. Bonnie loves creating art, reading, cruising the world, and being in natural surroundings. She has a deep connection with nature, with a special focus on trees and the unique characteristics of flora and fauna. Bonnie calls herself an Art Visionologist who wants to sustain her artistic expression and foster ongoing creativity. She works in all media and enthusiastically shares her passion for art, as she loves helping others discover their unique voice through creative visualization.

Please log in to **www.BonniesFolio.com** and find the Get In Touch section to receive special tips, exercises, and strategies.

Bonnie is available as a speaker, workshop leader, strategy innovator, Art Therapist, and motivator.

Contact the author through her website: **www.BonniesFolio.com** or email Bonnie directly at: **bonnie@bonniesfolio.com** to get scheduled for your next conference, group or team-building event, faculty workshop, art therapy session, or other training engagement. She is also available for one-to-one sessions with youth-adult, mental wellness discoveries. Visit the website for more information.

Also written by this Author, available on Amazon: *Seeing Creatively: How to Unlock Your Imagination*
https://www.amazon.com/Seeing-Creatively-Unlock-Your-Imagination/dp/B0DK5KK9LY

and

Awaken Your Inner Warrior: A Guide to Mindfulness through Meditative Neurographic Art
https://www.amazon.com/Awaken-Your-Inner-Warrior/dp/B0FTTQXY7D

Please leave a positive review on Amazon for these creative books! Thank you.

"A toolkit for the soul."
- Jack Canfield
Co-creator of the *Chicken Soup for the Soul* Series

ACKNOWLEDGEMENTS

I am fortunate to have my loving and supportive husband, Wayne, and a family who are not only close but the best at keeping life exciting! Thank you, Lindsey and Brendon Walker, and Brad and Rachel Wilczynski. I love and cherish you deeply.

I am also blessed to have such an enthusiastic love from Brody, Oakley, Blake, and Callie. You are what keeps me going!

Thank you to my *friends, followers, and loyal* readers. I wanted to give you something special. This is a mindful, calming way to encourage you to relax and leave stressors and worries behind, even for a little while. Breathe in and out slowly.

A special shout-out to Cristine Linder Deboni with Appenin Cabinets of Austin, who is a great inspiration and friend.

www.ingramcontent.com/pod-product-compliance
Lightning Source LLC
Chambersburg PA
CBHW080525030426
42337CB00023B/4634